Ron's Feeling Blue

Second edition

**Sheila Hollins, Roger Banks
and Jenny Curran
illustrated by Beth Webb**

Books Beyond Words/RCPsych Publications
LONDON

1

7

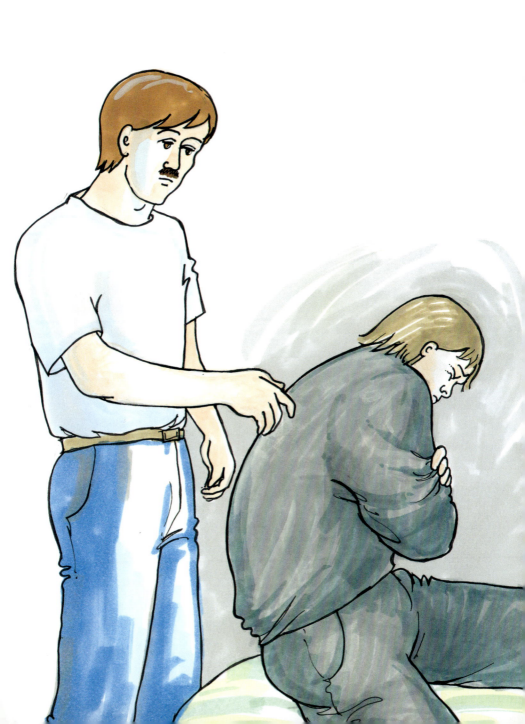

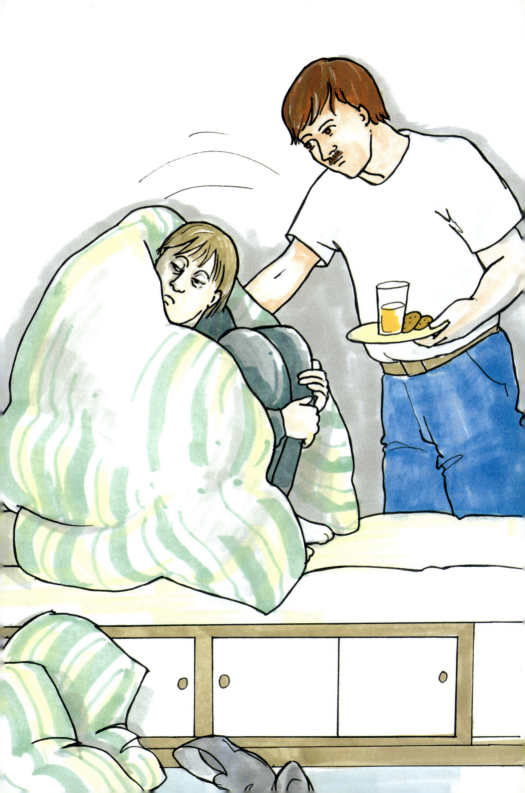

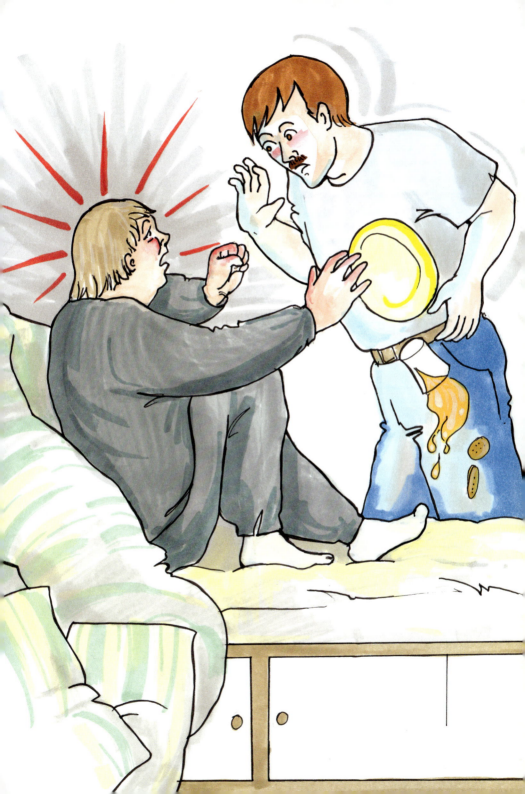

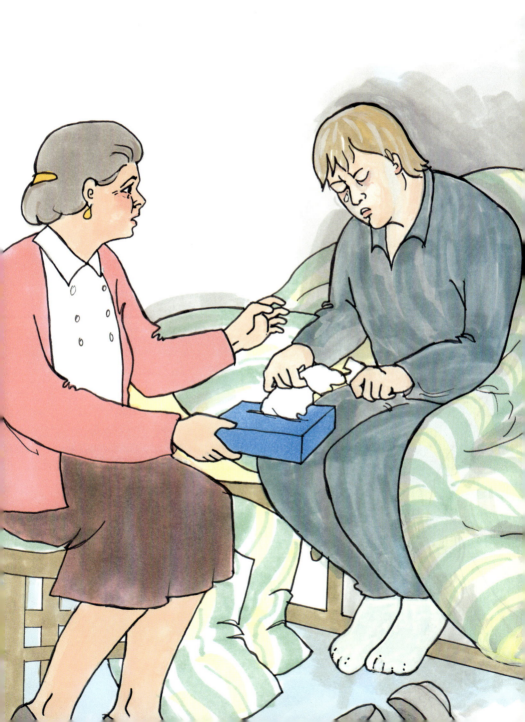

23

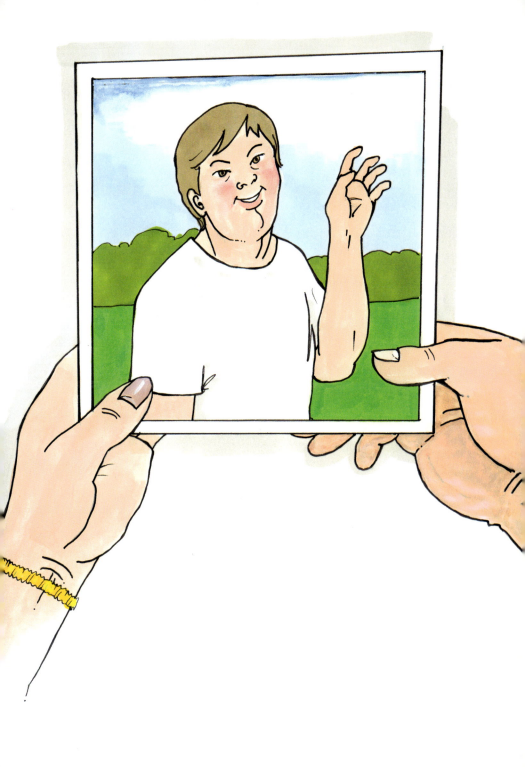

31

The following words are for people who want a ready-made story rather than tell their own

1. This is Ron. He is feeling blue/really down.
2. Jim wants to go out with Ron. Ron doesn't feel like it.
3. Jim wants to go swimming.
4. Ron doesn't want to swim.
5. Ron doesn't fancy his tea either.
6. Jim and Annie say there is swimming on the telly. Ron doesn't care.
7. Ron feels lots of things. He feels lonely and as if no one likes him. He feels dull and useless. He is really blue and fed up.
8. Jim is worried. He wants to help.
9. Jim tries to talk to Ron. Ron doesn't want to.
10. 'Go away!' Ron yells. 'Leave me alone!'
11. Ron doesn't want to get up. He feels lonely and tired all the time.
12. Ron is sad.
13. Jim brings Ron a drink and some biscuits.
14. Ron gets cross. 'Go away!' he shouts.
15. Jim phones the doctor. He tells her Ron feels bad.
16. The doctor comes. She knows Ron doesn't feel like talking. She just waits.
17. The doctor holds Ron's hand.
18. Ron begins to tell the doctor how he feels. She asks Ron to tell her more. She listens a lot.

19. Ron feels so sad, he cries.

20. Ron and the doctor talk some more.

21. The doctor has to go. She says, 'Goodbye, see you soon'.

22. Ron feels a bit better.

23. The doctor comes again on another day.

24. The doctor brings Ron this book. Ron and the doctor look at the book. Ron says, 'This book is about how I feel'. The doctor tells Ron he is depressed.

25. Ron looks at some photos. He remembers happy times.

26. Ron takes his photos to the doctor's.

27. He wants to talk about what made him happy and what made him sad.

28. Ron says, 'Look at this photo. I was really happy then'. Ron and the doctor talk a lot.

29. Ron begins to feel better after a while. He wants to go out with Jim.

30. Ron and Jim go swimming. It's fun!

31. Ron gives Jim some chocolate. It has been a great afternoon. Ron doesn't feel blue anymore.

Sometimes talking is not enough and the doctor may prescribe tablets. Pictures 32 and 33 are included for use when this happens.

32. The doctor tells Ron that he can take some pills to make him feel better.

33. Ron gets the pills from the chemist. He takes them every day.

33

Introduction

This book is about a young man with learning disabilities who becomes very sad and needs help to feel better.

Sadness and depression

Everyone can feel sad at any time in their lives, this is normal. There are things that happen, that people say or do, things that we think about that can make us all feel unhappy for a time. There are lots of words that people use for feeling this way: sad, unhappy, miserable, feeling blue, feeling down or low.

Although it is normal to feel this way, sometimes people may feel sad for longer than is usual and there may be other problems that come with this low mood.

When people are sad they find it difficult to see anything positive about their lives or their future. They may lose interest in doing things or may just not have the energy. They may cry a lot but they can also feel worried, unable to relax and irritable and impatient with others. For much of the time they may just feel empty, worthless or guilty. They can lose their appetite and have difficulty sleeping properly; though some people sleep or eat more than usual. Sometimes people may have physical symptoms such as stomach aches, bowel problems, headaches or other pains in the body and these can be related to the sadness they are feeling. Feelings of anxiety or panic are also common in people who are feeling sad.

If this sadness goes on for a long time, is quite severe and causes other problems – it becomes like an illness and doctors, psychiatrists and psychologists refer to this as 'depression'.

Some people are more likely to become depressed. It may come out of the blue or they may be someone who has a tendency to develop episodes of this low mood time after time. Sometimes you might be able to identify something that sets off this feeling.

In severe depression, a person can feel that life is meaningless and not worth living and have thoughts of wanting to harm themself or end their life.

Feelings are difficult things to describe and someone with learning disabilities or communication problems may not be able to tell other people how they feel and what they are thinking. Depression, therefore, shows in different ways such as changes in behaviour, losing the ability to do things or communicate with others, problems with control of bladder or bowel motions, angry outbursts, destructiveness or self-injury, and physical symptoms such as aches and pains.

Why do people with learning disabilities get sad or depressed?

People with learning disabilities will become sad and depressed for the same reasons as anybody else. There are some causes, however, that they might be more likely to encounter.

Loss and bereavement are commonly a cause for sadness and depression but not just when a family member or a friend dies. People who are supported by carers often have to cope with carers leaving; they may have been moved from one place to another in their lives, each time losing friends, carers, favourite and familiar activities and places. For an adult with learning disabilities who has lived with their parents all their life, when their parents die they not only have to face the loss of loved ones but they may be moved into care and away from their home, familiar possessions and routines.

People with learning disabilities, as they grow up, can become very aware of how they are viewed and treated differently to people without learning disability. They see other young people having opportunities, responsibilities and achievements in life that they themselves have not been able or allowed to have and this can lead to feelings of disappointment, anger and sadness.

Sometimes physical health problems may be underlying a person's low mood, for example an underactive thyroid gland, viral infections, heart problems, pain in the joints, diabetes. We know, however, that people with learning disabilities are less likely to have their physical illnesses recognised and to be given treatment than people who don't have a learning disability.

Neglect or physical and sexual abuse may lead to depression and people with learning disabilities are particularly at risk due to their dependency on others, difficulties in protecting themselves and not being able to speak up for themselves if abuse has happened.

Men and depression

Depression is said to be more common in women, however, it is possible that men get depressed just as often but are less likely to talk to other people about it. Men may show that they are depressed in other ways, such as being irritable or having sudden outbursts of anger or losing control. They may become more likely to take risks and to be aggressive towards other people. We also know that men are more likely to kill themselves when depressed, and to use drugs and alcohol to cope with their depression, which just makes matters worse. Men who are shy are more likely to get depression and one of the most common causes of depression for men is problems in a relationship or in their marriage. If a man has a job then stresses at work, the threat of losing his job or actually being made unemployed may be a cause.

What to do if someone is sad or depressed

The most helpful thing to do is to help the person to talk about how they are feeling, to talk about what is on their mind and what things are troubling them. Often people will avoid talking to each other about unhappy or difficult feelings or particular problems or worries.

Being helped to talk these things through with a friend, supporter or member of the family can help to make sense of these difficulties and can also lead to finding some practical solutions to problems that have been underlying the sadness and worry.

Giving people information about sadness and depression and how to overcome them can be a great help. There are many books and websites that deal with these issues and some are in a form that is easier to read. This book without words is an example of something that can be given to a person to look at and to talk about with a friend or carer or in a group with other people who may have similar problems.

If the sad feelings continue then it is advisable for the person to see their general practitioner (GP). The doctor will check for any possible health problems that could be contributing to the depression, and will investigate and treat these and also assist in finding other types of help if needed.

Because GPs usually only have short appointment times it is a good idea to explain when making a booking that more time may be needed. This is particularly important if the person with learning disabilities has communication problems and also if they are very nervous about seeing doctors. Extra time will help them to explain what has been happening and talk about things that it can be difficult to find the right words for.

It is always helpful for the person to be accompanied by someone who knows them well, who knows what sort of a person they usually are and who is able to explain how things have changed. It can also help to use pictures or drawings in trying to understand how someone has been feeling.

We must also remember that sometimes having someone else present can make it more difficult for the person to talk to the doctor. This may be the case when the person with learning disabilities wants to say things that might upset others, or if there is something that they want to keep private; people should always be allowed the opportunity to discuss their problems alone if they wish.

Help and treatment

For most types of depression, the GP will refer someone to see a counsellor or psychological therapist. The counsellor may see people at the doctor's surgery or they may have an office somewhere else. Counsellors offer people talking therapies, the opportunity to see them a number of times to talk about their feelings and problems that they have been having.

The counselling allows the person to talk about anything that they wish, including what has happened in their past. It will also focus on what thoughts they are currently having and how these might be making them feel worried or sad. For people with learning disabilities it is possible to adapt the therapy process to match the person's understanding or to help overcome problems in communication. Again, photographs or drawings or books like this one are very useful in helping people to understand each other better.

The counsellor, and the person they are helping, may decide that it would be helpful to meet with the person's family or carers to explain how the person has been feeling or particular problems that they have been having.

Occasionally, people may benefit from having a much longer course of talking therapy to work on difficult problems.

Although talking therapies are helpful for many people, they do not always improve the person's depression enough. In these cases, and for people who are severely depressed, a doctor can prescribe treatment in the form of antidepressant tablets or medicines; they can also give treatments for anxiety. These do not work for everybody and, if they do, it can take a few weeks of taking the treatment regularly before you notice a difference.

All tablets and medicines can have side-effects and treatments for depression and anxiety are no different; common ones are things like an upset stomach, diarrhoea, dizziness, difficulty sleeping or headaches. The doctor and/or pharmacist should give information on what kind of side-effects to expect, how most of them are not serious and may go away, and what to do if the side-effects are bad or causing significant problems and making the person feel worse. It is possible that changing to a different sort of treatment might be better.

If these treatments work, then it is important that the person does not stop taking them as soon as they stop feeling sad. It is necessary to keep taking the treatment for between 6 months and a year to make sure that the depression does not come back again.

People who do not get better with treatments from their GP, or whose depression is so bad that they are at risk through not eating or drinking enough or having strong thoughts about wanting to end their lives, can be referred to see a specialist. These specialists are called psychiatrists, and some have particular training and skills in working with people with learning disabilities;

they usually work in teams of health professionals including nurses and psychologists.

Some people have depression that comes back time and again. If this is the case they will usually be seen by a psychiatrist, who, with the other members of the team, will provide a combination of both talking therapies and medicines that try to stop these episodes of depression from happening again, or to make them more manageable.

Although sadness and depression are not a nice thing to have to go through, with the help of others this can often be a time for thinking about ways in which people want to change things in their lives. They can also deal with problems that have been around for a long time and think carefully about the changes they need to make that will help them to feel generally better about themselves and their life in the future.

Useful resources in the UK

(The information listed here was correct at time of publication.)

Organisations to contact for help and advice

Mencap's 'Getting it right' campaign (www.mencap. org.uk/gettingitright) helps people with learning disabilities get equal access to treatment. Mencap has worked with healthcare professionals and UK medical Royal Colleges to develop the 'Getting it right' charter, which lists the nine key adjustments that should be made for equal access to healthcare.

Mencap Learning Disability Helpline
If you have a problem accessing healthcare, you can contact this helpline on: 0808 808 1111

Typetalk: 18001 0808 808 1111
Text: 07717 989 029
Email: help@mencap.org.uk

MIND InfoLine: 08457 660 163 (local rate)
Available 9.15 am to 5.15 pm, Monday to Friday, for advice and support to service users.

Respond Helpline: 0800 808 0700
Supports people with learning disabilities, their carers and professionals, around any issue of trauma, including bereavement.

Samaritans: 08457 90 90 90 (local rate)
24-hour helpline for those feeling distressed,despairing or suicidal, or concerned about someone.
Email: jo@samaritans.org
Website: www.samaritans.org

Services in the UK

IAPT (Improving Access to Psychological Therapies)

In 2007 the English government made counselling available in primary care. IAPT was set up to find ways to improve the availability of psychological therapies, especially for people with depression or anxiety disorders. A document explaining how to access IAPT counsellors for people with learning disabilities is available at this website address: www.iapt.nhs.uk/wp-content/uploads/2009/02/83078-nhs-iapt-learning-dis.pdf

Community teams for people with learning disabilities (CTPLDs)

These are specialist multidisciplinary health teams that support adults with learning disabilities and their families by assessment, by supporting access to mainstream healthcare and by providing a range of clinical interventions, including counselling. Your GP or Social Services department should have the address of the local team.

Patient Advice and Liaison Service (PALS)

This service, known as PALS, has been introduced to ensure that the NHS listens to patients, their relatives, carers and friends, and answers their questions and resolves their concerns as quickly as possible. PALS also helps the NHS to improve services by listening to what matters to patients and making changes, when appropriate. Every hospital has a PALS service. You can contact them at your local hospital or via their website: www.pals.nhs.uk

Internet resources

Understanding Intellectual Disability and Health (www.intellectualdisability.info)

This website covers a wide range of physical and mental health issues for people with learning disabilities. It is designed for healthcare professionals and students but is widely used by family cares and support staff.

The Candle Project

The project offers guidance and resources to staff working with children and young people with learning disabilities and mental health issues. It makes links between a person's development and their culture, lifestyle, environment and mental health. A project resource is available for free online (www.clearthoughts. info/silo/files/294.pdf) or you can purchase it as a book or CD from the Association for Real Change (www. arcuk.org.uk, email: david.grundy@arcuk.org.uk).

Depression in Adults with Intellectual Disability – Checklist for Carers (www.cddh.monash.org/ research/depression)

This Australian website allows free access to a checklist designed for use by carers, in particular paid support staff. It is intended to be used on behalf of adults who are not able to convey their feelings and symptoms because of severe communication impairment. It is not a diagnostic tool but the information can help the GP when considering the possibility that depression may be present. Details of how the Checklist can be used are also on the website.

Valuing People Now (www.valuingpeoplenow.dh.gov. uk) offers advice about mental health issues for people with learning disabilities, their carers and families, and includes links to other websites with information.

What about us? (www.whataboutus.org.uk) supported some people with learning disabilities in mainstream schools to run action research projects about emotional well-being. They created an online resource which shares what they learned about how to support young people with learning disabilities.

Easy Health (www.easyhealth.org.uk) is a website created by Generate with easy to understand information about staying healthy and getting help with your health.

The following online resources are not specifically geared towards people with learning disabilities but might be useful to those with good literacy or their carers

First Steps (www.first-steps.org) offers a confidential Anxiety Actionline (tel. 0845 120 2916), audio relaxation CDs, leaflets on anxiety and depression and a Personal Recovery Course (membership is from £10 per year).

Living Life to the Full (www.livinglifetothefull.com) is an online course offering a range of free educational life skills resources based on cognitive–behavioural therapy (CBT) principles.

MoodGYM (www.moodgym.anu.edu.au) is an Australian website which offers free self-guided resources for overcoming depression, including learning modules, assessments, an interactive game and downloadable relaxation audio materials.

The Australian website **depressioNet (www. depressionet.org.au)**, created by people with personal experiences of depression, aims to empower people to make informed choices and find solutions to the challenges of living with depression.

The Black Dog Institute (www.blackdoginstitute.org. au) in New South Wales, Australia, is a not-for-profit, educational, research, clinical and community-oriented facility offering specialist expertise in depression and bipolar disorder.

Beyond Blue (www.beyondblue.org.au) and **Youth Beyond Blue (www.youthbeyondblue.com)** are designed to help adults and young people with problems such as depression and anxiety.

Young Minds (www.youngminds.org.uk) work to improve the mental health of children and young people.

Written information

Mind booklets *Understanding Depression* and *Understanding Anxiety* can be purchased from www. mind.org.uk/shop/booklets

The **Mental Health Foundation** booklet *Dealing with Depression* (2006) helps people to recognise symptoms of depression and suggests remedies, including diet, exercise, medication and counselling.

It can be downloaded for free from www.mhf.org.uk/publications.

Pavilion Publishing has many training resources available for purchase (www.pavpub.com) about mental health and learning disabilities, including DVDs such as 'Mental Health in Learning Disabilities: A Training Resource' and books such as *Mental Health in Learning Disabilities: A Reader*.

An **Anxiety UK** booklet *The Carer's Guide to Anxiety* can be purchased at the Anxiety UK online shop: www.anxietyuk.org.uk/products/booklet/carers-guide-to-anxiety

A **Foundation for People with Learning Disabilities** booklet *All About Feeling Down* can be downloaded free from their website (www.learningdisabilities.org.uk/publications) or call Customer Services on 020 7803 1101.

CHANGE (www.changepeople.co.uk) has an illustrated booklet on depression for people with learning disabilities – *Depression. What is Depression? What Causes Depression? What Treatments are Available?* You can order it from Change, Unit 41, Shine, Harehills Road, Leeds LS8 5HS. Telephone: 0113 388 0011.

Anxiety Disorders: The Caregivers – Information for Support People, Family and Friends by Kenneth Strong. ISBN 1590790561. Available from www.amazon.co.uk

Exploring Your Emotions Manual by A. Holland, A. Payne and L. Vickery. A set of 30 full-colour photographs illustrating common emotions that can be used in educational and therapeutic settings to help people with learning disabilities learn about their own feelings and the relationship between emotion and behaviour. Available from www.amazon.co.uk

Related titles in the Books Beyond Words series

Sonia's Feeling Sad (2011) by Sheila Hollins and Roger Banks, illustrated by Lisa Kopper. This story is about a woman who is depressed and shows the ways that she is helped to feel better.

When Mum Died and *When Dad Died* (2004) are two books by Sheila Hollins and Lester Sireling, illustrated by Beth Webb. Both books take an honest and straightforward approach to death and grief in the family. The pictures tell the story of the death of a parent in a simple but moving way.

When Somebody Dies (2003) by Sheila Hollins, Noelle Blackman and Sandra Dowling, illustrated by Catherine Brighton. This book tells the story of two people who experience bereavements and the different support they are given.

Going to the Doctor (1996) by Sheila Hollins, Jane Bernal and Matthew Gregory, illustrated by Beth Webb. This book illustrates a variety of experiences which may occur during a visit to the GP. These include meeting the doctor, having one's ears syringed, a physical examination, a blood test, a blood pressure check and getting a prescription.

Going to Out-Patients (2009) and *Going into Hospital* (1998) are two books about what happens to people in hospital. Feelings, information and consent are all addressed.

Some other titles in the Books Beyond Words series

Am I Going to Die? (2009) by Sheila Hollins and Irene Tuffrey-Wijne, illustrated by Lisa Kopper. This is a story about a man who is terminally ill, told in an honest and moving way.

I Can Get Through It (1998) by Sheila Hollins, Christiana Horrocks and Valerie Sinason, illustrated by Lisa Kopper. This story shows how a woman is helped to get through the experience of being abused with the help of a counsellor or therapist.

Jenny Speaks Out (2005) by Sheila Hollins and Valerie Sinason, illustrated by Beth Webb. Jenny moves to a new home in the community and her carers realise she was abused by her father. The story shows how the warmth and trust of her carer and friends begin a healing process which will bring hope and a fresh start for Jenny. This book may enable a person with learning disabilities or mental health problems to open up about their experience of sexual abuse.

Getting on with Cancer (2002) by Veronica Donaghy, Jane Bernal, Irene Tuffrey-Wijne and Sheila Hollins, illustrated by Beth Webb. This book tells the story of Veronica who has various treatments for cancer, including radiotherapy, chemotherapy and surgery. It deals honestly with the unpleasant side of treatment and ends on a positive note.

George Gets Smart (2003) by Sheila Hollins, Margaret Flynn and Philippa Russell, illustrated by Catherine Brighton. George's life changes when he goes running with his friends and workmates and he learns the importance of keeping clean and smart.

Michelle Finds a Voice (1997) by Sheila Hollins and Sarah Barnett, illustrated by Denise Redmond. Michelle has cerebral palsy and cannot communicate what she is feeling to the people who might help her. Michelle and her carers explore various solutions to overcome these difficulties, including the use of signing, symbol charts and electronic communication.

Falling in Love (1999) by Sheila Hollins, Wendy Perez and Adam Abdelnoor, illustrated by Beth Webb. This love story follows the relationship between Mike and Janet from their first date through to deciding to become engaged to be married.

Go to www.rcpsych.ac.uk/bbw for full details of all the titles available in the Books Beyond Words series.

You can purchase the books online or by writing to: Book Sales, Royal College of Psychiatrists, 17 Belgrave Square, London SW1X 8PG. Tel: 020 7235 2351 ext: 6146. Fax: 020 7245 1231.

Acknowledgements

With grateful thanks to members and clients of the Wandsworth Community Team, and Sue Lord, Tricia Stewart, Freda Macey and Emily Westlake, for their help in creating the story and pictures; and to British Telecom for providing financial support for the first edition of this book. The second edition has been further developed with the help of Emily Westlake and Dorothea Duncan.

Authors

Sheila Hollins is Professor of Psychiatry of Learning Disability at St George's, University of London, and sits in the House of Lords. She is a past President and an Honorary Fellow of the Royal College of Psychiatrists.

Roger Banks is a Consultant in the Psychiatry of Learning Disability with Betsi Cadwaladr University Health Board. He is a Fellow of the Royal College of Psychiatrists and an Honorary Fellow of the Royal College of General Practitioners.

Jenny Curran is a Fellow of the Royal Australian and New Zealand College of Psychiatrists and Senior Consultant Psychiatrist in Developmental Disability Psychiatry with the Department for Families and Communities, South Australia.

Beth Webb is an artist with a background in psychology and sociology who specialised in alternative communication media. She has pioneered the use of emotional colour and mime in her illustrations for the Books Beyond Words series.